D1503913

THE SHAPING AND RESHAPING OF EARTH'S SURFACE™

Igneous Rocks
and the Rock Cycle

Joanne Mattern

The Rosen Publishing Group's
PowerKids Press™
New York

Published in 2006 by The Rosen Publishing Group, Inc.
29 East 21st Street, New York, NY 10010

First Edition

Editor: Melissa Acevedo
Book Design: Ginny Chu

Photo Credits: Cover and title page © David Muench/Corbis; p. 4 (inset) © Corbis; p. 4 © Larry Fellows Arizona Geological Survey; pp. 6, 7 Ginny Chu/Rosen Publishing; pp. 8 (center inset), 11, 14 (insets) U.S. Geological Survey; p. 8 © Jim Sugar/Corbis; p. 8 (top) © Roger Ressmeyer/Corbis; p. 10 (bottom) © Jonathan Blair/Corbis; p. 10 (top) © Corbis; p. 12 © NASA/Roger Ressmeyer/Corbis; p. 13 © Caron Philippe/Corbis Sygma; pp. 14, 17 (right) © Gary Braasch/Corbis; p. 16 © Richard Cummins/Corbis; p. 17 (left) © Dr. Richard Busch; p. 18 © Adam Woolfitt/Corbis; p. 19 © Bettmann/Corbis; p. 20 © David Muench/Corbis; p. 21 © Reuters/Corbis.

Library of Congress Cataloging-in-Publication Data

3 0691 00163832 9

Mattern, Joanne, 1963–
  Igneous rocks and the rock cycle / Joanne Mattern.— 1st ed.
    p. cm. — (The shaping and reshaping of earth's surface)
  Includes index.
  ISBN 1-4042-3196-X (lib. bdg.)
  1. Rocks, Igneous—Juvenile literature. 2. Geochemical cycles—Juvenile literature. I. Title. II. Series.

  QE461.M438 2006
  552'.1—dc22

                                            2004029326

Manufactured in the United States of America

Contents

This picture was taken at the Kilauea Volcano in Hawaii. It shows lava cooling down and hardening into igneous rock.

The word "igneous" comes from a Latin word that means "fiery." Igneous rocks have this name because they are formed from hot liquid magma.

Right:
Igneous rocks are very important to Earth. This igneous rock from Arizona cooled in columns. This happens when the rocks pull away from each other during the cooling process.

Igneous Rocks

What Are Igneous Rocks?

Rocks are a major part of Earth's surface and our lives. All rocks are made of matter called minerals and belong to one of three different groups. These groups are igneous rocks, sedimentary rocks, and metamorphic rocks.

Igneous rocks can form underground when hot liquid magma is trapped in small pockets. There it cools and hardens into igneous rocks. Igneous rocks can also form on Earth's surface. Volcanoes erupt and force magma onto the surface, where it cools and hardens into igneous rocks. The formation of these rocks is key to the rock cycle.

Igneous rocks can form underground when hot liquid magma is trapped in small pockets. There it cools and hardens into igneous rocks.

Igneous Rocks in the Rock Cycle

The rock cycle is the process by which rocks are changed from one form to another. The rock cycle is able to provide Earth continuously with new rocks through the breaking down of old rocks and the hardening of magma to form new ones.

The rock cycle starts when hot magma rises to the surface of Earth. Once on the surface, the magma cools and hardens into igneous rocks. Over time wind and water wear down these igneous rocks. In the end they become sedimentary rocks. These rocks can be pushed under the crust through movements such as earthquakes. The

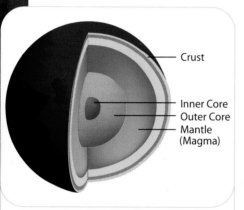

Crust

Inner Core
Outer Core
Mantle
(Magma)

Earth is made up of layers. The top layer, called the crust, is made of rock. Under the crust is the mantle, a layer of hot liquid called magma. Below the layer of magma is Earth's core. It is made up of two layers. The outer layer is made up of melted metals. The inner layer is a ball made out of solid metal.

sedimentary rocks under the surface, as well as the igneous rocks that have formed underground, are changed into metamorphic rocks through heat and

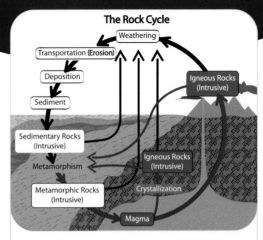

The Rock Cycle

Weathering

Transportation (Erosion)

Deposition

Sediment

Sedimentary Rocks (Intrusive)

Metamorphism

Metamorphic Rocks (Intrusive)

Igneous Rocks (Intrusive)

Igneous Rocks (Intrusive)

Crystallization

Magma

This diagram shows the changing of old rocks into new ones through the process of the rock cycle. Igneous rocks form when magma cools and hardens.

pressure. Magma melts these metamorphic rocks and is then pushed to the surface or becomes trapped within Earth. When magma cools it forms new igneous rocks, below and above ground. The rock cycle begins again.

The rock cycle starts when hot magma rises to the surface of Earth. Once on the surface, the magma cools and hardens into igneous rocks.

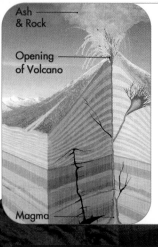

Ash
& Rock

Opening
of Volcano

Magma

This diagram
of a volcanic
eruption shows
the path that
the magma
takes when
being forced
out onto
Earth's surface.

When a volcano
erupts, it sends out
lava and igneous
rocks. The black sand
beaches in Greece,
Hawaii, New Zealand,
and Scotland were
created from the
igneous rocks that
were thrown from
nearby volcanoes
after eruptions.

Right:
*This volcano is called
Kilauea and is in
Hawaii. Kilauea
erupted in 1984.*

How Igneous Rocks Are Formed

Volcanoes

Earth's crust is broken into giant pieces called plates that float on top of liquid magma. At times the plates rub against each other, causing a fault line to appear in the crust. Fault lines are weak places in Earth's crust. Volcanoes form when magma flows into these fault lines. Heat and pressure inside Earth force the magma up through the fault line and out onto Earth's surface. Magma cools into rock and over time can build up to form a volcanic mountain. As the volcano continues to erupt and send out lava, the lava hardens to form igneous rocks.

Earth's crust is broken into giant pieces called plates that float on top of liquid magma.

Cooling

When igneous rocks form through the process of cooling deep inside Earth, they are called intrusive. Intrusive igneous rocks form when a pool of magma becomes trapped in a small pocket under Earth's crust. This trapped magma cools slowly and after thousands of years, it hardens into igneous rock.

An igneous rock called granite formed Mount Rushmore in South Dakota thousands of years ago. The rock of Mount Rushmore was formed when it cooled underground but was later lifted to the surface by movements such as earthquakes.

When magma cools slowly, as in the case of the intrusive igneous rock, the minerals that are inside the rock form large crystals. If you look at an igneous rock called granite, you can often see colorful

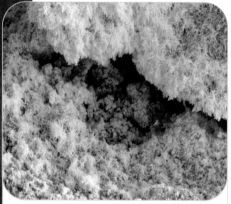

This picture was taken in 1981 in Italy. It shows crystals on some igneous rocks that were created by a volcano in the area.

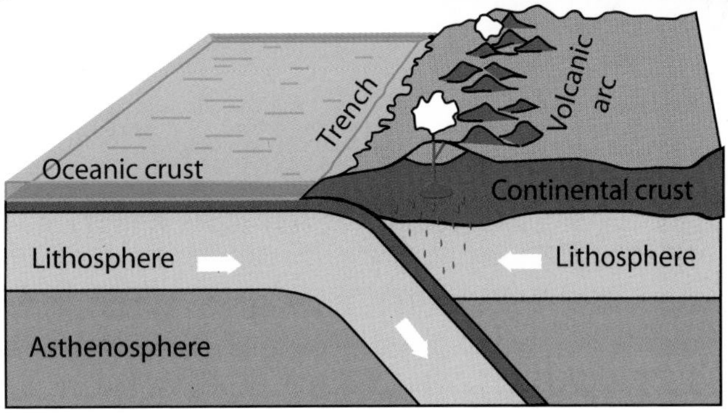

Trench
Volcanic arc
Oceanic crust
Continental crust
Lithosphere
Lithosphere
Asthenosphere
Oceanic-continental convergence

This diagram shows two of Earth's plates meeting. Intrusive rocks that have cooled inside Earth are pushed to the surface in this way.

spots. These are the crystals of different minerals inside the rock.

Magma that cools fast forms small crystals. An example of this is the intrusive basalt rock. If magma cools very fast, crystals do not have a chance to form at all. An example of this is obsidian rock. The formation and size of the crystals affect what the rock looks and feels like.

Intrusive igneous rocks form when a pool of magma becomes trapped in a small pocket under Earth's crust.

Space Rocks

Some igneous rocks form in outer space, far away from our planet. Planets such as Mercury, Venus, and Mars are made of igneous rocks, just as most of Earth is. Sometimes pieces of these planets break off and join asteroids in their travels through space. These pieces are mostly made up of igneous rocks and are called meteorites. Meteorites sometimes hit planets while traveling through space. Each year about 19,000 meteorites land on Earth. Most are very small, but some are large enough to harm houses or cars. Scientists study the meteorites that hit Earth and learn many

The dark parts of the Moon are made up of an igneous rock called basalt. This rock formed when meteorites and other space matter hit the Moon with so much force that they broke the surface. Lava would ooze out of these breaks. Once the lava cooled, it formed the basalt rock.

things about the other planets in our solar system. For example, we know that meteorites from Mars are made of an igneous rock called pyroxenite.

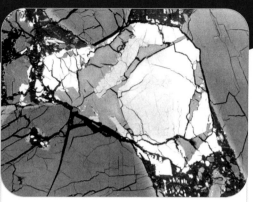

This picture shows a piece of a meteorite under a microscope. This meteorite came from Mars. It is made up of a rock called pyroxenite.

Even our Moon is made of igneous rocks! When we look at the Moon from Earth, some of the igneous rocks that make it up look white. These rocks are called anorthosite, norite, and troctolite. The dark parts of the Moon are made up of an igneous rock called basalt.

Meteorites sometimes hit planets while traveling through space. Each year about 19,000 meteorites land on Earth.

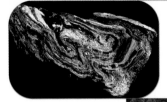

Rhyolite, a light-colored rock, forms from rhyolitic lava.

This basaltic lava is hardening to form basalt rocks.

Lava sometimes spreads out, covering a lot of land. An area of Oregon, Washington, and Idaho called the Columbia Plateau is made of basalt rock that formed millions of years ago when a large amount of lava cooled.

Right:
This picture of a part of the Columbia Plateau was taken in 1983.

Kinds of Igneous Rocks

Volcanic Rocks

Igneous rocks are split into two groups. The first group, volcanic, or extrusive, rocks, is formed when lava cools after a volcanic eruption. These rocks usually have small crystals because the lava cools quickly. The hardened lava forms a layer of igneous rock around the volcano, making it taller.

There are two types of lava. Basaltic lava flows quickly and smoothly, forming volcanoes with sloping sides. Rhyolitic lava is thicker and flows slowly, creating volcanoes with steep sides. Rhyolitic eruptions are strong enough to toss lava and rock miles (km) away from the volcano.

The hardened lava forms a layer of igneous rock around the volcano, making it taller.

Obsidian, Pumice, and Basalt

There are many kinds of extrusive rocks. One of these rocks, obsidian, can form when basaltic or rhyolitic lava comes in contact with water. When the lava pours into a body of water, it cools very quickly and has no crystals. This means that obsidian is smooth and shiny with a glassy texture. It is usually black but can also be dark green or reddish brown. Obsidian is used in making jewelry and as an ornamental stone for carvings.

The Giant's Causeway in Northern Ireland is made of thousands of basalt columns. Some of these columns are more than 20 feet (6 m) high! The causeway formed when basaltic lava cooled into basalt rock. Basalt rock often forms in columns.

Pumice is another kind of extrusive rock. It forms from rhyolitic eruptions. When this rock is formed, the lava cools so quickly that the air has no time to escape and the rock forms tiny air-filled holes.

Obsidian has tiny crystals. For this reason, it is hard and breaks easily.

This is a picture of a cracked pumice rock.

These air-filled holes make pumice the lightest rock on Earth. Pumice is so lightweight that it can float in water. It is used in many household cleaning products and to wash jeans. The pumice beats the cloth and gives it a faded look.

Basalt rocks form from basaltic eruptions. Basalt rocks are usually black and feel rough. They cover much of ocean floors because of underwater volcanic eruptions. Basalt can be thousands of feet (m) thick and can stretch over many miles (km). Sometimes after basalt cools, it breaks and forms six-sided columns. The Giant's Causeway in Northern Ireland is made of basalt columns.

Basalt can be thousands of feet (m) thick and can stretch over many miles (km). Sometimes after basalt cools, it breaks and forms six-sided columns.

Plutonic Rocks

The second type of igneous rock is called plutonic, or intrusive. Intrusive rock forms from magma that cools in small pockets below Earth's surface. Intrusive rocks are forced up to the surface by earthquakes and volcanic eruptions.

Intrusive rocks cool very slowly. This slow cooling process allows large crystals to form. These crystals are so large that they can be seen without a microscope. Intrusive rocks have a rough texture, and they also come in many colors. Some of the rocks have spots or a speckled appearance because of the large crystals inside them.

This lion in Venice, Italy, was made of porphyry rock. Porphyry is a kind of igneous rock that is both intrusive and extrusive. These rocks cooled below Earth's surface but were forced to the surface by volcanic eruptions before they finished hardening.

18

Intrusive rocks are used by people for many different things. Granite, the best-known igneous rock, is an intrusive rock that is used to build walls and buildings. The walls of the Empire State Building in New York City are made from granite.

Construction on the Empire State Building began back in 1930. The people who planned the building wanted to use a rock that was stable and strong. For this reason granite was used to build the walls.

Intrusive rocks have a rough texture, and they also come in many colors.

Granite, Gabbro, and Kimberlite

Granite is the most common intrusive rock. Granite can be many different colors, including gray, white, pink, or red. It is often spotted with crystals made from the minerals quartz, feldspar, and mica. Granite can be used in many different construction projects because it is very hard and strong. The oldest known rock in the world is made of granite. It is nearly four billion years old!

One of the reasons granite is so widely used is because it can be found almost anywhere! This granite rock is from Texas.

Gabbro is another intrusive igneous rock that is used for building. It has large crystals and looks like granite, but gabbro is darker in color. Sometimes it looks blue or green. Gabbro has different minerals than granite has.

Kinds of Igneous Rocks: Granite, Gabbro, and Kimberlite

Important metals such as nickel and platinum are sometimes found in gabbro.

This is a picture of a kimberlite mine. Diamonds often form near kimberlite, so the rocks are mined in open pits, such as the one above.

Kimberlite is an unusual intrusive igneous rock that forms in long pieces that look like pipes. These pieces push up through the ground. This rock is usually blue, green, or black in color. Kimberlite forms very deep under Earth's surface, about 93 miles (150 km) underground, where there is much heat and pressure. This pressure and heat often cause diamonds to form near kimberlite.

Kimberlite is an unusual intrusive igneous rock that forms in long pieces that look like pipes.

The Importance of Igneous Rocks

People use igneous rocks in many different ways. Native Americans and people who lived in ancient times used obsidian to make tools, masks, weapons, jewelry, and even mirrors. People all over the world have looked for diamonds and other precious stones in or near kimberlite to make jewelry. Scientists also use igneous rocks to study Earth. These rocks can teach us much of what we need to know about volcanoes and their formation. They can also show us what is going on deep inside Earth.

The rock cycle has been changing Earth for millions of years. Igneous rocks are an important part of that cycle. As magma continues to harden into igneous rocks, the rock cycle will continue for many more years to come!

asteroids (AS-teh-roydz) Small bodies made of rock and iron that travel around the Sun.

crystals (KRIS-tulz) Patterns of many flat surfaces inside minerals.

earthquakes (URTH-kwayks) Shakings of Earth's surface caused by the movement of pieces of land called plates that run into each other.

extrusive (ik-STROO-siv) Having to do with a type of igneous rock formed when lava cools on the surface of Earth.

igneous rocks (IG-nee-us ROKS) Hot, liquid, underground minerals that have cooled and hardened into rocks.

intrusive (in-TROO-siv) Having to do with a type of igneous rock formed when magma cools and hardens under Earth's surface.

jewelry (JOO-ul-ree) Objects worn for decoration that are made of special metals, such as gold and silver, and prized stones.

lava (LAH-vuh) A hot liquid made of melted rock that comes out of a volcano during an eruption.

metamorphic rocks (meh-tuh-MOR-fik ROKS) Rocks that have been changed by heat and heavy weight.

meteorites (MEE-tee-uh-ryts) Rocks from outer space that reach Earth's surface.

minerals (MIN-rulz) Natural elements that are not animals, plants, or other living things.

plates (PLAYTS) The moving pieces of Earth's crust, the top layer of Earth.

plutonic (ploo-TAH-nik) Having to do with igneous rock formed when magma hardens under Earth's surface. Another name for intrusive.

sedimentary rocks (seh-deh-MEN-teh-ree ROKS) Layers of gravel, sand, silt, or mud that have been pressed together to form rocks.

texture (TEKS-chur) How something feels when you touch it.

volcanoes (vol-KAY-nohz) Openings in the surface of Earth that sometimes shoot up a hot liquid rock called lava.

Index

Web Sites

Due to the changing nature of Internet links, PowerKids Press has developed an online list of Web sites related to the subject of this book. This site is updated regularly. Please use this link to access the list:
www.powerkidslinks.com/sres/igneous/